Drawing Pictures with Shapes

By Wendy Body

Contents

Longman

Circle Drawing 1

1   Draw a big circle.

2 Draw a small circle on top of the big circle.

3 Draw two triangles on the small circle.

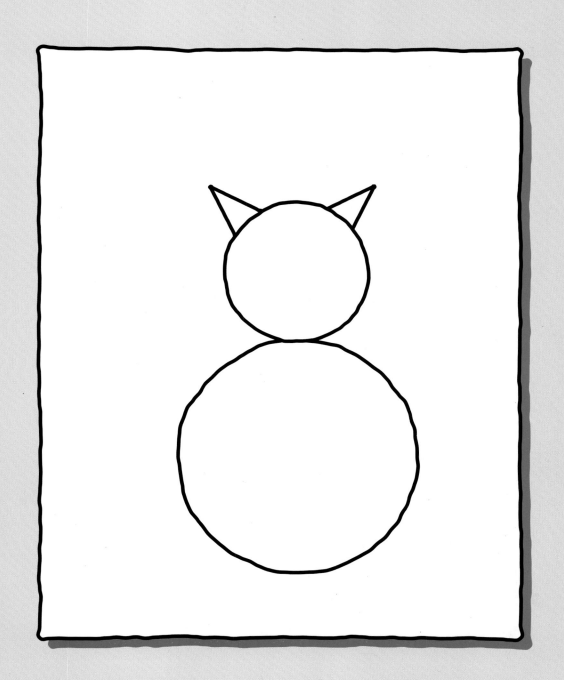

What does it look like?

A cat!

4 Make your drawing into a cat.

5 Colour it in.

Circle Drawing 2

1 Draw a big circle.

2 Draw a small circle on top.

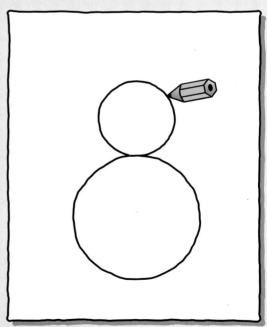

3 Draw a hat on the small circle.

What does it look like?

A snowman!

4 Make your drawing into a snowman.

5 Colour it in.

Triangle dog

1   Draw a triangle for the head.

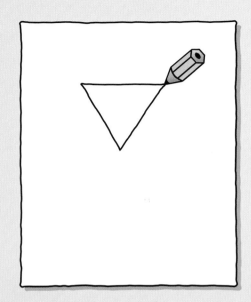

2   Draw two small triangles for the ears.

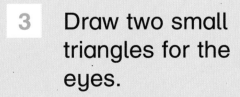

3   Draw two small triangles for the eyes.

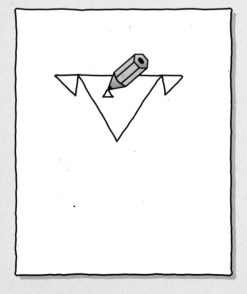

4 **Draw a big long triangle for the body.**

5   Draw two small triangles for the legs.

6   Draw one small triangle for the tail.

7 Now colour in your dog and give it a name.

Triangle Mouse

1 Draw a big triangle for the body.

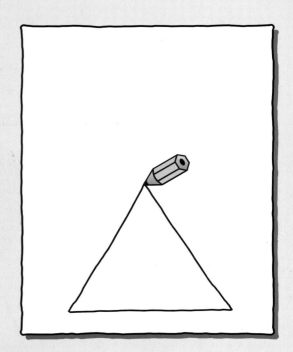

2 Draw a long triangle for the head.

3 Draw two small triangles for the ears.

4 Draw two very small circles to make the eyes.

5 Draw a small circle for the nose.

6 Draw some lines for the whiskers.

7 Draw a long curly tail.

8 Now colour your mouse and give it a name.

Rectangle Robot

1 Draw a big rectangle for the body in the middle of the paper.

2 Draw a small rectangle on top of the big one to make the head.

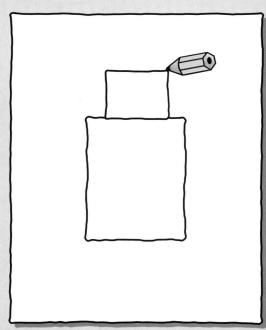

3 Draw two small rectangles to make the eyes and a long one to make the mouth.

4 Draw two long rectangles to make the robot's arms.

5 Draw two smaller rectangles to make the hands.

6 Draw two long rectangles to make the robot's legs.

7 Draw two smaller rectangles to make the feet.

8 Colour your robot and give it a name.

Triangle Girl

1 Draw one big triangle for the body in the middle of the paper.

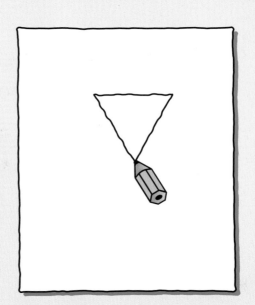

2 Draw a smaller triangle on top of the big one to make the head.

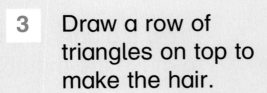

3 Draw a row of triangles on top to make the hair.

4 Draw two very small triangles to make the eyes and one to make the nose.

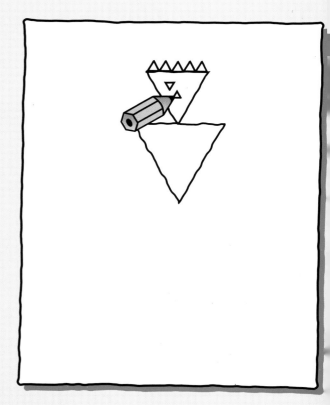

5 Draw a bigger triangle to make the mouth.

6 Draw two long triangles to make the girl's arms.

7 Draw two smaller ones to make the hands.

8 Draw a triangle to make a skirt.

9 Draw two triangles to make the girl's legs.

10 Draw two smaller ones to make the feet.

11 Colour your girl and give her a name.